SUNRISE POINT ELEMENTARY
LIBRARY MEDIA CENTER

ARCHAEOLOGICAL MYSTERIES

SECRETS OF POMPEII

BURIED CITY OF ANCIENT ROME

BY TIM O'SHEI

Consultant:
Richard S. Williams
Associate Professor, Emeritus
Department of History
Washington State University
Pullman, Washington

CAPSTONE PRESS
a capstone imprint

Edge Books are published by Capstone Press,
1710 Roe Crest Drive, North Mankato, Minnesota 56003
www.capstonepub.com

Copyright © 2015 by Capstone Press, a Capstone imprint. All rights reserved. No part of this publication may be reproduced in whole or in part, or stored in a retrieval system, or transmitted in any form or by any means, electronic, mechanical, photocopying, recording, or otherwise, without written permission of the publisher.

Library of Congress Cataloging-in-Publication Data
O'Shei, Tim.
Secrets of Pompeii : buried city of ancient Rome / by Tim O'Shei.
    pages cm.—(Edge Books. Archaeological mysteries)
Includes bibliographical references and index.
Summary: "Describes the archaeological wonder of Pompeii, including discovery, artifacts, ancient peoples, and preservation"—Provided by publisher.
ISBN 978-1-4765-9916-8 (library binding)
ISBN 978-1-4765-9925-0 (paperback)
ISBN 978-1-4765-9921-2 (eBook pdf)
1. Pompeii (Extinct city)—Juvenile literature. 2. Vesuvius (Italy)—Eruption, 79—Juvenile literature. I. Title.
DG70.P7O84 2015
937'.72568—dc23
                                                                              2014007002

Developed and Produced by Focus Strategic Communications, Inc.
    Adrianna Edwards: project manager
    Ron Edwards: editor
    Rob Scanlan: designer and compositor
    Karen Hunter: media researcher
    Francine Geraci: copy editor and proofreader
    Wendy Scavuzzo: fact checker

Photo Credits
Alamy: Heritage Image Partnership Ltd., 19, LatitudeStock, 11; Deborah Crowle Illustrations, 5, 21; Focus Strategic Communications Inc., 3, 4–5 (back), 6, 7 (back), 15, 21 (back); Getty Images: National Geographic, 23; iStockphotos: edella, 28–29, Flory, 16, 26–27; Library of Congress, 4; Newscom: EPA/Andy Rain, 12; Shutterstock: Alfio Ferlito, 9, Antonio Abrignani, 7, mary416, 18, Porojnicu Stelian, cover, 1, Sadik Gulec, 13; SuperStock: DeAgostini, 20; Thinkstock: Photos.com, 24–25

Design Elements by Shutterstock

Printed in the United States of America in Stevens Point, Wisconsin
042014   008092WZF14

TABLE OF CONTENTS

CHAPTER 1	DIG A RIVER, FIND A CITY!	4
CHAPTER 2	BUILDINGS AND RELICS	6
CHAPTER 3	PEOPLE	14
CHAPTER 4	DOWNFALL	20
CHAPTER 5	PRESERVATION	26

GLOSSARY	30
READ MORE	31
CRITICAL THINKING USING THE COMMON CORE	31
INTERNET SITES	32
INDEX	32

CHAPTER ONE

DIG A RIVER, FIND A CITY!

A team of workers was digging a tunnel in southern Italy. They were working several miles south of the city of Naples. Scoop by scoop, they shoveled up dirt. Then—clack! Suddenly they stopped. They had hit something big and hard. What had they found?

Their boss, **architect** Domenico Fontana, told the workers to dig deeper. The object they had hit was a brick wall. With a bit more digging, they uncovered more brick walls and even saw paintings on them.

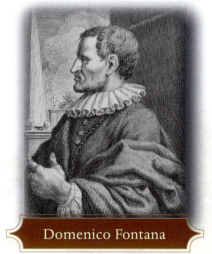

Domenico Fontana

The workers didn't know what they had found, but they had stumbled upon the ancient city of Pompeii. By the time Fontana's crew found it in 1599, Pompeii was just a name in old stories.

architect—a person who designs buildings and advises in their construction

Long before, Pompeii was a rich, busy Roman city. It was located just 5 miles (8 kilometers) from a volcano called Mount Vesuvius. More than 1,500 years earlier, the volcano exploded with a terrifying **eruption**—and Pompeii vanished.

The **artifacts** were interesting, but the workers weren't there to discover an ancient city. They were supposed to be digging a tunnel. So Fontana had the men cover up the findings and move on with their work. Nobody made a big deal of it at the time, but Pompeii had been found!

eruption—the action of a volcano suddenly throwing out rock, hot ash, and lava with great force

artifact—an object used in the past that was made by people

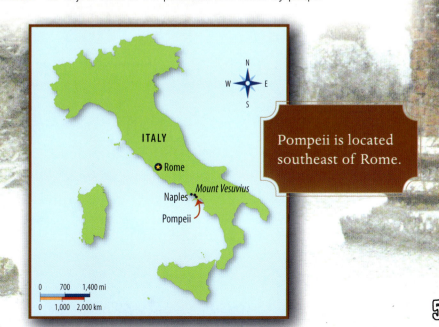

Pompeii is located southeast of Rome.

CHAPTER TWO

Buildings and Relics

In the years after the accidental discovery of Pompeii, more people stumbled across the remains of the city. This often happened when they were digging for water. But nobody made plans to search Pompeii until the mid-1700s. At that time a team of Spanish archaeologists started to **excavate** the city. Back then most searches were little more than treasure hunts. These adventurers were trying to find artwork for the king, not learn about the past. But after the Spanish archaeologists' dig, more people became interested. Some came with shovels, hoping to dig out their own treasures. Others were hoping to use the artifacts to learn about the past. They wanted to know—what was life in Pompeii actually like? Eventually, archaeologists would find out. But that didn't happen in a big way for a very long time.

excavate—to dig in the earth

Artifacts such as pottery tell about life in Pompeii.

Target for Thieves

Pompeii has been a target of thieves over the years. Some of the buildings have holes in their walls. Robbers made those holes as they dug into the volcanic ash that buried Pompeii. They then chipped their way into the buildings to take jewelry and artwork. Robberies are still happening. In 2003 thieves broke into the Pompeii bakery and stole art from the wall. They left a half-eaten pizza inside!

Digging Deep

The first big excavation of Pompeii came in 1860. That year Italian archaeologist Giuseppe Fiorelli and his team started digging deep into the city. Fiorelli uncovered long-buried remains of the once-bustling city, including buildings and roads. He kept detailed notes on everything his team found. So have many archaeologists who followed him. Because of archaeologists like Fiorelli, visitors to Pompeii today can walk the ancient city's streets.

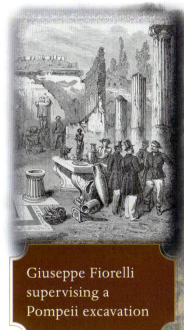

Giuseppe Fiorelli supervising a Pompeii excavation

Highly Decorated Homes

Pompeii was smothered in ash from the Mount Vesuvius eruption. In some cases the city was buried under many feet of ash. The ash helped preserve the buildings and artifacts under it. That is why so many buildings, both large and small, are still standing.

Some houses were so small and basic that they barely let in any outside light. Others were as grand as palaces. They had 20, 30, or even 40 rooms. In larger homes the floors, walls, and sometimes ceilings were decorated with carvings, tiles, and **mosaics** of animals and people. In one house is a mosaic of a dog. In another is a **fresco** painting of people doing everyday things, such as buying bread at a bakery.

On the floor of Pompeii's largest home, the House of the Faun, is a large mosaic that shows a warrior named Alexander the Great in battle. The mosaic is made of about 1 million tiny tiles.

mosaic—a picture or pattern made from small, colored shapes; pieces of colored glass can be used to make mosaics

fresco—a large picture painted on wet plaster

Archaeological Fact

On the floor of the entrance to the House of the Tragic Poet, a mosaic shows a sharp-toothed black and white dog. The words "Cave Canem" appear. That means "Beware of the dog!"

Alexander the Great was a military leader who conquered much of the known world during his lifetime. The original mosaic from Pompeii is now in a museum.

WATER, WATER EVERYWHERE

It was common for homes in Pompeii to have a large **atrium** inside the doorway. The ceiling above the atrium was open, letting in both sunlight and rain. The rainwater would fall into a basin and be used in the house. Eventually, an **aqueduct** system was built to carry running water to public baths, fountains, and a few homes of the very rich.

atrium—a large, open space in a home or building

aqueduct—a large bridge built to carry water from a mountain into the valley

Beautiful Buildings

Pompeii's buildings are often stunning, with marble walls, detailed bronze statues, and tall columns. Many of these were built around the Forum, a large, open area. People came to the Forum to socialize, shop at the nearby markets, and make business deals. The three temples near the Forum held religious ceremonies. There were government buildings where politicians made laws. There were also the Roman public law courts where criminals were put on trial.

For fun people went to the theater for plays or shows. The largest gathering spot was the **amphitheater**, a stadium-like building in the southeast corner of the city. The amphitheater could seat more than 20,000 people to watch fights between **gladiators**. These fighters were usually criminals or prisoners who were forced to battle, often to the death.

As they watched and cheered from their seats in the stands, people could see Mount Vesuvius looming. They probably never guessed that one day it would destroy their city.

amphitheater—a large, open-air building with rows of seats in a high oval around an arena; in Ancient Roman times, gladiators often fought in amphitheaters

gladiator—a fighter who was forced to battle, often to the death

BLOODY BATTLES

Each gladiator battle usually lasted 10 to 15 minutes. A gladiator won when his opponent could fight no more. Often the crowd was asked to decide whether the losing gladiator should live or die. Many times, the crowd decided to let the loser live. A few gladiators were skillful enough to earn their freedom. The best ones became big celebrities.

the ruins of the amphitheater of Pompeii

Jewelry, Statues, and Food

The artifacts discovered at Pompeii have helped us learn more about life in the ancient city. In larger, richer homes, archaeologists have found artwork, glassware, pottery, and perfume bottles. The jewelry is heavy and highly decorated. For example, archaeologists found a gold armband in the shape of a coiled snake. They also found gold earrings, bronze statues, and emeralds bunched like grapes. There was an ivory statue of the Hindu goddess of beauty. That statue probably means somebody in Pompeii was trading goods with someone in India.

Archaeologists have also found preserved food, such as fruits and vegetables. In one bakery dozens of loaves of bread were still there, seemingly ready to eat!

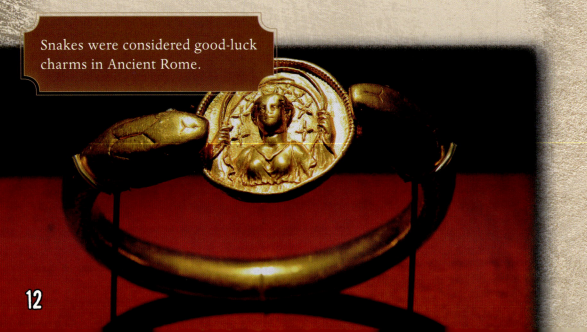

Snakes were considered good-luck charms in Ancient Rome.

Weapons and Armor

The Pompeii building known as the House of the Gladiators was full of battle gear. There were bronze helmets with images of warriors and bronze shields with images of gods and olive branches. A small dagger had a handle made of bone.

Carvings and drawings on the walls of the House of Gladiators showed more weapons. Some showed gladiators who were lightly armed, with just a shield and a dagger or small sword. Others showed gladiators carrying a three-pronged spear called a trident and a heavy net.

Gladiators fought not only people but also wild animals.

CHAPTER THREE

PEOPLE

Pompeii has been compared to a time capsule—a container used to store old things to be opened in the future. Why? The artifacts found there tell us how the Ancient Romans lived.

In 1860 Giuseppe Fiorelli and his men started excavating Pompeii. They found places where people had been trapped in the ash. The flesh and bones had rotted away, leaving hollow spaces. Fiorelli had his men pour plaster into the open spaces. When the plaster dried, they chipped away the ash. What they had, then, was a cast of the person in the exact position in which he or she died. The detail was amazing. Teeth, clothing, and even hair can been seen on some of the casts.

ARCHAEOLOGICAL FACT

Pompeii's wealthier residents owned slaves. Although the slaves weren't free, they did get to do many of the same things as their masters. For example, they ate the same food, washed in the same baths, and used the same bathrooms as their owners.

By studying these casts and the artifacts found with the remains, archaeologists have learned much about the people of Pompeii. For example, people who wore wide belts were slaves. Each belt had the name of the slave's owner. The cast of one woman was found with a small silver and gold statue of the god Mercury. Ancient Romans believed Mercury helped people travel safely. Clearly this woman was religious. There were 100 people who died in an outdoor gymnasium. One of them was carrying a wooden box with tweezers, sharp knives, and other tools. Archaeologists believe he may have been a doctor trying to help injured people.

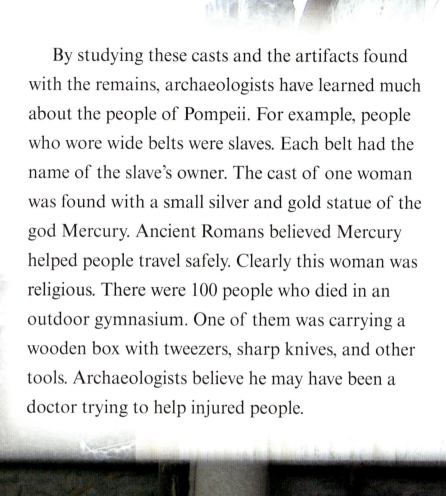

Plaster casts of Pompeii victims show what they were doing when they were buried in the ash from Mount Vesuvius' eruption.

Clues of Daily Life

Archaeologists use two major clues for figuring out how the people of Pompeii lived. Those clues are the artifacts they left behind and the pictures on the walls. For example, we know many people of Pompeii were rich because they had fancy jewelry and large homes. Pictures on the walls tell us about their daily habits.

Pictures on the walls show what Pompeians wore, the furniture they used, and how they decorated their homes.

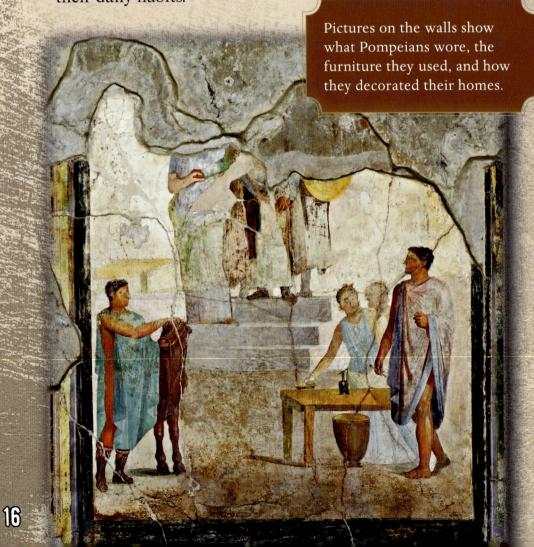

Writing on the Wall

Many homes in Pompeii, even the fancy ones, were bare on the outside. People often covered the plain walls with writing called graffiti. Sometimes the messages were serious, such as asking people to vote for someone running for office. Other messages were more playful, like "Auge amat Allotenum." That means "Auge loves Allotenus."

People raised crops near Pompeii. The mix of volcanic stone and ash that comes from a volcano like Vesuvius eventually becomes very fertile soil. This rich soil allowed people to grow a variety of crops, which were sold at the city markets. People could buy onions, cabbage, almonds, cherries, beans, and more. Pompeii citizens also produced wine, olive oil, and a fish sauce, called garum, to trade with people in other regions. The city was known for more than its food, though. The wool from the sheep on farms was used to create fabric that became popular.

Daily Bathing

The people of Pompeii liked to be sociable. But their idea of entertainment was different from what is popular today. People went to public bathhouses. These buildings had separate entrances so that men and women had their own bathing areas. Inside they could choose to take a hot, warm, or cold bath. Often people chose two—or all three! Inside the baths, people might sit for hours, chatting with one another. The richer citizens could also get food, massages, and haircuts.

an Ancient Roman public bathhouse

Afterward they might be hungry. There were several places around Pompeii that served food. These places had stone counters with holes for storing food. These early restaurants were called thermapolia. They were similar to modern buffets. Pompeii also had several taverns where people could buy food and drinks.

Sports

Not everybody ate after bathing. The athletic, younger people may also have headed to a gymnasium, which was called a palaestra. They would exercise, run, or play ball games. They might even compete in track-and-field sports. From the many paintings and statues of muscular male athletes found in Pompeii, it's clear that being strong and competitive was important.

For entertainment people would often head to a theater to see a play or to the racetrack to see events such as chariot racing. Some of these spectacles would go on for hours or even days.

Chariot racing was a popular sport in Pompeii.

CHAPTER FOUR

DOWNFALL

August 24, AD 79, was the beginning of the end for Pompeii. The day began with nervous donkeys pulling at their chains. Dogs were barking, seemingly for no reason. But when the people looked in the direction of Mount Vesuvius, they couldn't believe what they saw! A huge cloud of smoke was shooting from the top of the volcano into the sky.

The people of Pompeii were shocked to see clouds of smoke coming from Mount Vesuvius.

Earthly Action

Earth's crust is made up of **seismic** plates that move. When these collide, they trigger earthquakes and volcanic eruptions. Italy is located near the spot where two plates meet. That is why earthquakes are common in Italy.

One week before the eruption of Vesuvius, Pompeii was hit with an earthquake. Thousands of people left the city when that happened. That was a good decision. By fleeing then, they saved their lives.

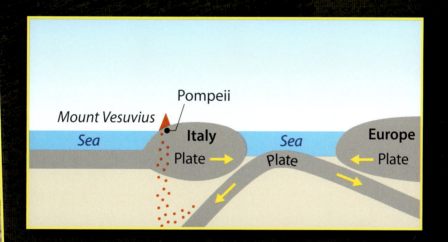

Volcanoes can erupt when seismic plates slam into each other. If one plate slides under the other, hot melted rock, called magma, can form in the Earth. If the magma rises and reaches the volcano's top, an eruption occurs.

seismic—caused by or relating to an earthquake

FLEEING THE CITY

Mount Vesuvius hadn't erupted for 1,500 years. Most of the Pompeians didn't even know it was a volcano. They were probably confused by the dark, cloudy smoke rising from it on August 24. But many realized the best idea was to get out.

If the sight of Vesuvius smoking wasn't enough to convince them to leave, what happened next probably was. By mid-morning, rocks and ash were raining from the sky. As the hours went on, the rocks got bigger and the ash turned thicker.

By mid-afternoon the roads were clogged with fleeing people. Hundreds were crushed as the crowd raced to escape the city. Soon the air was so full of ash that people could not breathe. By early evening, the ash blanketed Pompeii in darkness. Still, the worst was yet to come.

DANGER ON THE WATER

From about 15 miles (24 kilometers) away, a naval commander named Pliny the Elder was watching the disaster in Pompeii. Wanting to help, he set sail for the city. His teenage nephew, Pliny the Younger, stayed back to watch.

The younger Pliny later wrote letters describing what he saw. The sea was thrashing. Waters pulled back from the shores, leaving hundreds of sea creatures to die on the beach. This also meant that people fleeing Pompeii by water probably met deadly waves on their escape.

The ash and gas in a volcanic surge can be as hot as 1,800°F (1,000°C).

THE SURGE

As the evening wore on, the rocks and ash stopped falling on Pompeii. Some of the people who had been hiding inside buildings came out. They may have thought the worst was over—but they were wrong.

Around midnight the giant column of volcanic gas that had been shooting out of Vesuvius collapsed inward. That sent a surge of super-hot gas and ash hurtling down the side of the mountain. This fast-moving surge swept through Pompeii, instantly killing anyone in its path. Buried under many feet of rock and ash, Pompeii was gone.

ARCHAEOLOGICAL FACT

When Mount Vesuvius erupted in AD 79, thousands of people were killed. Estimates vary, but experts put the total at about 2,000 killed in the two days of the eruption.

CHAPTER FIVE

Preservation

The artifacts of Pompeii have taught us about the Ancient Romans' lifestyle. The discoveries aren't over, though. Archaeologists are still working in the region around Pompeii. In recent years, for example, they discovered 54 skeletons in the cellar of a **villa**.

Pompeii Today

More than 2 million people visit Pompeii every year. Thanks to the work of archaeologists for more than 200 years, the city is remarkably well preserved.

villa—a large, fancy house, especially one in the country

Because Pompeii is a popular tourist site, scientists do have concerns. The ancient city is fragile. In 2010 the gladiators' building collapsed. Italian officials are concerned about the wear and tear that such large crowds are having on Pompeii. The World Monuments Fund and United Nations have Pompeii on their lists of important archaeological sites.

tourists at Pompeii

ERUPTION ... AGAIN?

Pompeii may have a bigger problem. Mount Vesuvius is still active. It has erupted at least 30 times since the disaster at Pompeii. Most of those eruptions were not huge. But some scientists still call Vesuvius the world's most dangerous volcano. Many of them believe Vesuvius is due for another major eruption.

Mount Vesuvius overlooks the modern city of Naples.

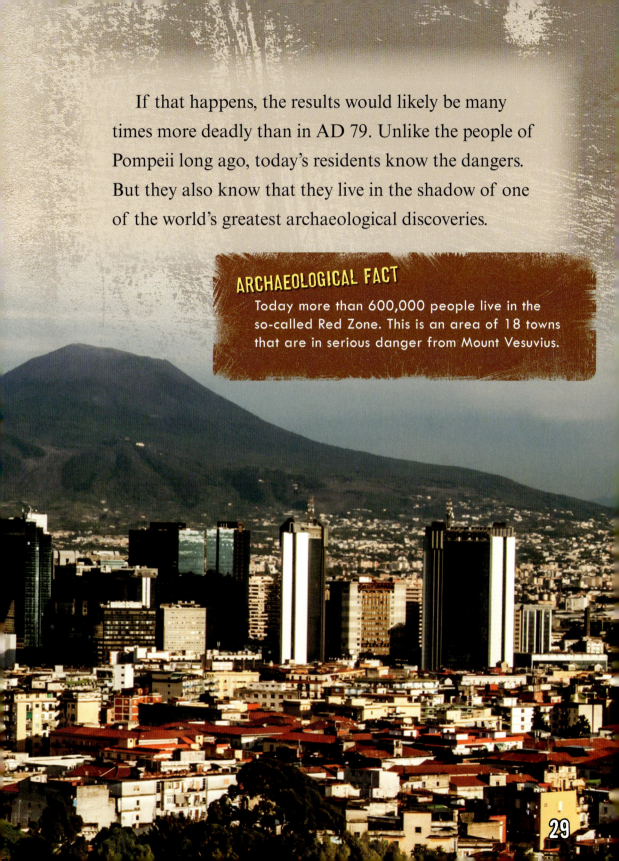

If that happens, the results would likely be many times more deadly than in AD 79. Unlike the people of Pompeii long ago, today's residents know the dangers. But they also know that they live in the shadow of one of the world's greatest archaeological discoveries.

ARCHAEOLOGICAL FACT

Today more than 600,000 people live in the so-called Red Zone. This is an area of 18 towns that are in serious danger from Mount Vesuvius.

GLOSSARY

amphitheater (AM-fuh-thee-uh-tuhr)—a large, open-air building with rows of seats in a high oval around an arena; in Ancient Roman times, gladiators often fought in amphitheaters

aqueduct (AK-wuh-duhkt)—a large bridge built to carry water from a mountain into the valley

architect (AR-ki-tekt)—a person who designs buildings and advises in their construction

artifact (AR-tuh-fact)—an object used in the past that was made by people

atrium (AY-tree-uhm)—a large, open space in a home or building

eruption (i-RUHP-shuhn)—the action of a volcano suddenly throwing out rock, hot ash, and lava with great force

excavate (EK-skuh-vayt)—to dig in the earth

fresco (FRES-koh)—a large picture painted on wet plaster

gladiator (GLAD-ee-ay-tuhr)—a fighter who was forced to battle, often to the death

mosaic (moh-ZAY-ik)—a picture or pattern made from small, colored shapes; pieces of colored glass can be used to make mosaics

seismic (SIZE-mik)—caused by or relating to an earthquake

villa (VIL-uh)—a large, fancy house, especially one in the country

READ MORE

Collins, Terry. *Escape from Pompeii: An Isabel Soto Archaeology Adventure*. Graphic Expeditions. Mankato, Minn.: Capstone Press, 2011.

Costain, Meredith. *The End of Pompeii*. Ancient Civilizations. New York: PowerKids Press, 2013.

Malam, John. *Pompeii and Other Lost Cities*. Lost and Found. Irvine, Cal.: QED Publishing, 2011.

Wagner, Heather Lehr. *Pompeii*. Lost Worlds and Mysterious Civilizations. New York: Chelsea House, 2011.

CRITICAL THINKING USING THE COMMON CORE

1. Reread the main text on page 6 as well as the sidebar Target for Thieves on page 7. What are two reasons people excavated Pompeii? Are these good reasons? Explain your thinking. (Key Ideas and Details)

2. On page 18 the text states "The people of Pompeii liked to be sociable. But their idea of entertainment was different from what is popular today." Do you agree or disagree with this statement? Use specific examples from the text to support your answer. You may also use other resources for more evidence. (Integration of Knowledge and Ideas)

3. Look at the sidebar on page 21 and reread pages 28 and 29. What are the realities facing people living near Mount Vesuvius today? Would you be comfortable living there? Why or why not? (Key Ideas and Details)

INTERNET SITES

FactHound offers a safe, fun way to find Internet sites related to this book. All of the sites on FactHound have been researched by our staff.

Here's all you do:

Visit www.facthound.com

Type in this code: 9781476599168

Check out projects, games, and lots more at www.capstonekids.com — Super-cool stuff!

INDEX

agriculture, 12, 17
Alexander the Great, 8, 9
amphitheater, 10, 11
artifacts, 5, 6, 7, 8, 12, 14, 15, 16, 26

bathhouses, 18

chariot racing, 19

earthquakes, 21

Fiorelli, Giuseppe, 7, 14
Fontana, Domenico, 4, 5

gladiators, 10, 11, 13
graffiti, 17

jewelry, 7, 12, 16

mosaics, 8
Mount Vesuvius, 5, 8, 10, 15, 17, 20, 21, 22, 24, 25, 28

plaster casts, 14, 15
Pliny the Elder, 24
Pliny the Younger, 24
pottery, 6, 12

Red Zone, 29

seismic plates, 21
slaves, 14, 15
sports, 19

tourists, 26, 27
treasure hunters, 6, 7

United Nations, 27

volcanoes, 5, 17, 20, 21, 22, 24, 25, 28

World Monuments Fund, 27

30229016548496
937 OSH
O'Shei, Tim.
Secrets of Pompeii :
buried city of ancient Rome /